TABLE TALK SAMPLER

31 DAYS OF STORIES, QUOTES, AND QUESTIONS TO SPARK CONVERSATION AT THE DINNER TABLE

KIMBERLY FLETCHER, EDITOR

MOMS FOR AMERICA

Copyright © 2012 by Homemakers for America

Copyright © 2025 by Moms for America

All rights reserved.

ISBN: 979-8-9900769-8-3

No portion of this book may be reproduced in any form without written permission from the publisher or author, except as permitted by U.S. copyright law.

Contents

How to get the Most from this Booklet	V
The Power of Family Dinner Hour	1
1. Day 1~ Share a Story	31
2. Day 2~ Share a Story	34
3. Day 3~ Share a Quote	35
4. Day 4~ Ask a Question	37
5. Day 5~ Share a Story	38
6. Day 6~ Share a Quote	41
7. Day 7~ Share a Story	42
8. Day 8~ Share a Quote	44
9. Day 9~ Ask a Question	46
10. Day 10~ Share a Story	47
11. Day 11~ Share a Bible Verse	49

12. Day 12~ Ask a Question   51
13. Day 13~ Share a Story   52
14. Day 14~ Ask a Question   54
15. Day 15~ Share a Story   55
16. Day 16~ Share a Quote   61
17. Day 17~ Share a Story   62
18. Day 18~ Ask a Question   64
19. Day 19~ Share a Story   65
20. Day 20~ Share a Bible Verse   67
21. Day 21~ Ask a Question   69
22. Day 22~ Share a Story   70
23. Day 23~ Share a Story   73
24. Day 24~ Share a Quote   76
25. Day 25~ Share a Story   77
26. Day 26~ Share a Bible Verse   81
27. Day 27~ Ask a Question   83
28. Day 28~ Share a Story   84
29. Day 29~ Ask a Question   89
30. Day 30~ Share a Story   90
31. Day 31~ Share a Quote   93

How to Get the Most from This Booklet

The Table Talk Sampler is put together in two parts. The first part is an introduction to the concept of Family Dinner Hour. The second part is a list of 31 days of stories, quotes, questions, and Bible verses to spark conversation during family dinner.

To get the most from this booklet, it is highly recommended that you take the time to read through the first part before taking advantage of the second part.

On each of the days listed, there is a question, quote, story, or Bible verse to share. In some cases, there are additional resources listed and suggestions to guide the discussion. We know each family is different and has children of various ages, but this Sampler was put together with that in mind. While some of the questions may seem too advanced for a 3-year-old and some stories may seem too juvenile for a 14-year-old, most of the suggestions offered can be adapted to any age. In addition, we have included supplementary resources and suggestions on many of the days to provide alternatives to meet the needs of your own family.

For the best experience, we suggest you take a few minutes before dinner, or even earlier, in the day to read that day's topic. This will give you time think on the topic and read through any additional resources suggested.

While this is a great resource to get you started in creating amazing family dinner discussions, it is just a beginning. There are several resources you can use to keep the discussions going, which we have highlighted in the introduction. We will also continue to add to the resources on our website to help keep you inspired and your family talking.

Most of all, just sit back, relax, and enjoy the magic of family dinner. The memories you make and seeds you plant will last a lifetime. The relationships you foster will have a profound effect on your children, and the love you nurture around that humble table will have a lasting influence that will be felt for generations to come.

THE POWER OF FAMILY DINNER HOUR

KIMBERLY FLETCHER

"All great change in America begins at the dinner table."

~Ronald Reagan

FAMILY DINNER USED TO be a fairly common thing. The institution of family was still highly respected in those days, and family togetherness filled the TV Guide line-up with shows like *Little House on the Prairie*, the *Waltons*, and the *Brady Bunch*. Of course, there were other *not* so family friendly shows as well, but they were few and played later in the evening. The 6:00 to 9:00 timeframe was dedicated to family viewing, acknowledged and respected as sacred family time, which began with family dinner. Streets, backyards, and playgrounds that had filled with children the moment school let out suddenly cleared at 5:30 as the children headed home to have dinner with their families.

Things are much different today. TV lineups are filled with shows like *Pretty Little Liars*, and the overloaded schedules families juggle have devolved Family Dinner Hour from 'sit and talk' to 'grab and run'.

With so many options in fast-food dining and takeout, family dinner has become almost obsolete; after all, with all the things grabbing at our attention and filling our day, who has time to make dinner? And even if we do sit down to KFC or Chinese Take-out, what do we talk about?

Family conversation has been reduced to senseless chatter boasting the last level achieved in Pokemon Go, the new posts on Facebook, and pleas for those new designer shoes our kids just *have* to have. This is, of course, between all the texts to and from friends and sharing all the new jokes posted on our iPhones. But fast-food and unlimited technology aren't the only things vying for our precious family time. Media has become a huge competitor for our time with easy access to virtually everything with hundreds of TV channels just a thumb click away.

Unfortunately, while our TV viewing options have quadrupled in quantity over the last few decades, they have plummeted in quality on a grand scale. Show content is shallow and weak, family relationships are presented as dysfunctional, violence is commonplace (often graphic), and what would have been considered X-rated at theaters thirty years ago is now splashed all over TV screens—and not only for primetime viewing. With all the cable options now available, adults and children alike can watch soft porn, adult situations, and outright nudity at virtually any time of the day.

What's being called "family viewing" these days is downright criminal. Only fifteen years ago, children enjoyed the Disney afternoon with *Tailspin* and *Chip n Dale's Rescue Rangers*. Today, the Disney channel is filled with shows that present parents as weak and incompetent while children run amuck. And anyone ever thought the Family Channel could pass as something "family" is absurd. That's probably why they changed it to "Freeform."

With so many distractions and negative influences in our children's lives, and the constant blatant attack on the institution of family, a return to Family Dinner Hour is not only well overdue, it is vital to the success of a civilized society and the preservation of liberty itself.

The Power of Family Dinner Hour

From the very founding of our nation, when the Pilgrims first landed on Plymouth Rock, the center of America was families. Families worked together, learned together, prayed together, and yes, they ate together. It was around the dinner table that families shared their thoughts, addressed concerns, and discussed news and current events in their community.

It is where children learned proper etiquette, received their first lessons in social civility, and developed the skills of conversation.

As America grew, the family dinner table became the place where liberty and tyranny were discussed at length; where Thomas Paine's pamphlet Common Sense was introduced into family conversation, and where the Federalist Papers were read, discussed, and even debated. It was in the home that the principles of liberty were fostered and nurtured, and the dinner table became a venue for sharing revolutionary ideas. Today the dinner table is a place to drop book bags on the way to the TV or the Wii. What a tragedy to American culture.

Laurie David, author of "The Family Dinner," states in her book that research has proven that everything we worry about as parents—from drugs to alcohol, promiscuity to obesity, academic achievement, and just good old nutrition—can all be improved by the simple act of eating and talking together around the table.[1] Just think of all the disputes that could be settled, the dreams that could be developed, the virtues that could be nurtured, and the relationships that could be fostered if we took the time to sit down and have dinner together as a family. We could solve so many problems that ail our nation right there at the dinner table.

Perhaps you feel it is oversimplifying to suggest that simply eating dinner together as a family could heal our nation. Perhaps you are right, but consider this: America didn't begin with a government, it began with families who *formed* a government—the most revolutionary government the world had ever seen. That government didn't originate in a palace, an ornate capital building, or a grand cathedral. It began around the fireplaces and dinner tables of rugged cabins in a vast wilderness thousands of miles from any established civilization. If the greatest government experiment in human history could begin there—in the home, with the family—shouldn't that be the place where we concentrate our greatest efforts to preserve it?

Home is the great conservator of good, the seedling place of virtue, and the origin of all civilization. The words uttered and doctrines taught around the fireside and dinner table are the influences which shape the destinies of empires. The laws of a nation are merely the outward reflection of the principles and morals established in the home.

As C. E. Sargent stated in his book <u>Our Home</u>, "It is the influences of home that live in the life of kingdoms, while parental counsel repeats itself in the voices of republics. We would impress upon the minds of our readers this grand truth, and would that we might thunder it into the ears of all mankind, that a nation is but a magnified home!"[2]

If we want to know the destiny of our nation, if we want to catch a glimpse of the future of civilization, all we need to do is look in our homes. What we see in the homes of America today is what our nation will be tomorrow. Are you scared yet?

So, what will our future look like? *We* are the ones who decide. If our children can't even sit down together to have dinner as a family and talk to each other, how can they sit in the halls of Congress and have substantive discussions on the issues which will impact the entire free world?

When our founding families left their homeland they brought with them their virtues, their principles, and the Bible. As the stories of the heroes and patriots from the Bible were shared, young hearts were touched, morals were established, and the principles of liberty, virtue, and civility were fostered. Heavy emphasis was put on manners as the colonists desired to prove that they could be just as civilized as their European counterparts. Our founding families realized the great importance of manners as they dictated how one would, could, and should act within society. It was at the dinner table that these manners were nurtured and developed.

Through the discussions and time spent in Family Dinner Hour, children learned the proper ways to engage in conversation and behave socially—not only with speech, but with their body movements and gestures as well. They learned a tilt of the head or roll of the eyes had meanings which communicated a message to others. As families gathered together, parents and children nurtured love and learned how to communicate effectively. They learned how to organize their thoughts, define their message, and convey the ideas they intended through their words *and* their actions.

Young children developed powerful skills at the dinner table. It wasn't just a meal the family ate together, it was a family experience where children learned to form their thoughts into words of expression which would influence and inspire others. As the generations passed, it would be those children who would become the writers of world changing documents, such as the author of a little pamphlet entitled "Common Sense"; who would give impassioned speeches that would be immortalized for centuries; who would leave bloody footprints in the snow at Valley Forge; who had the courage to stand before the hangman's noose and humbly declare, "I regret that I have but one life to give to my country."

It was those children who would take a seemingly uninhabitable wilderness and by the sweat of their brow, with unwavering conviction and steadfast hearts, raise up a mighty nation which would become the hope of all the world. *That* is the power of Family Dinner Hour!

Okay, I'm sold. Where do I start?

While the notion of family dinner seems a simple concept, anyone who has attempted to sit down at the table together as a family and have a relaxing meal with decent conversation knows it isn't easy. And I'm sure you're wondering why I keep referring to it as the family dinner "hour". After all, any decent American can finish a meal in 15 minutes these days, right? While it is true the actual eating part may only take 15 minutes, when you include the preparation and clean-up it can easily take a whole hour. Just think of all the amazing conversations you can have during that time.

We have compiled a list of basic things you should know when planning your family dinner adventure. And for those of you who are already family dinner regulars, the information, ideas, and suggestions in this booklet may help to make the experience even better. We'd love to hear your ideas and success stories too—as well as those challenges you've faced and how you worked through them and/or overcame them. We're all in this together.

Seven Basic Steps to Get You Started

One: Make a Commitment

Anytime you start something new it requires commitment to keep it going. This means more than just committing to the family dinner, it also means putting in the time and planning needed to fulfill that commitment. And it is important that both parents are on board. For this reason, it is highly advised that husband and wife council together when starting Family Dinner Hour so they can discuss together how it works best for their family. When the children see that both parents are committed to the idea, they will be much more likely to support it and make the commitment as well.

This in no way means you can't do it if you are a single mom. It just means you get all the buy-in on your own. You can even get grandparents on board.

Since Family Dinner Hour is centered around dinner, food is definitely something that should be considered. You will need to decide, based on your own family's situation, how the food part of the family dinner will work. A good home-cooked meal is ideal, but eating together is the most important thing, so if KFC is what works best for you, then KFC it is. Once you form the habit, you can start branching into the cooking part.

Once you've committed to starting Family Dinner Hour, that commitment will give you the strength and fortitude to keep going during those frustrating times when you wonder if the whole thing is really worth the hassle. I promise it *will* get better. All new things take time to work. You may not see the results the first week, or even the first month, but you will see results, and you will be pleasantly surprised when they come.

Remember, family dinner isn't just a meal we eat at a designated time of day; it is time we take *out of our day* to spend together as a family. Not only are relationships nurtured and strengthened by sharing this time together, studies prove that eating dinner together as a family actually makes us smarter, healthier, and happier. You will witness the proof at your own table.

Two: Clear Your Calendar

While family dinner hour sounds like a fairly simple idea, in today's hustle and bustle world, it's rarely easy. But personal experience attests that when you schedule something it is much more likely to happen. We have a saying in our family, "If it's not on the calendar it doesn't happen." Our children grew up with this phrase ringing in their ears, and they have come to realize that there is a big message between those few words. They know that if they need a ride somewhere or have an activity they want to attend, it has to be on the calendar. That way, everyone knows about it—most especially Mom—and we, as a family, are able to make any arrangements or accommodations to ensure that the transportation and needed support is available.

This has been a great way for our family to learn to plan and respect each other's time and resources. It has also taught me to be respectful of my children's time. Just because I have older children doesn't mean I should assume I always have a babysitter when I need one. Our children have lives too. They have interests and commitments. So when we decide to implement something that will involve everyone's time, it is important that we take the time to sit down as a family to determine the best time that will work for everyone and allow us the greatest chance for success in having everyone together for family dinner.

It is also important to be flexible. Not everyone will be able to attend family dinner every day, and there will be some days where 'eat and run' is the only option. That's okay, and it doesn't at all constitute failure. It just means you get the opportunity to be creative.

I remember one day when things were exceptionally crazy for our family. We had dentist appointments right after school, my daughter had an activity to go to right after that, and our sons had soccer games that evening. Not even the Crockpot plan was going to work that day. So, we sat down as a family the day before and spent a few minutes going through the schedule for the next day. I packed a dinner for my daughter and picked up a couple rotisserie chickens and some fruit on the way to drop her off. Then we headed to the soccer fields where my husband met us and we had a picnic dinner on the sidelines as we cheered on the kids and watched the game. It wasn't at the table, but it was definitely a Family Dinner Hour.

Three: Prepare for Dinner

Preparing for dinner doesn't just include making the evening meal. There is so much more that goes into it. And just as it is important to put family dinner on the calendar to ensure it happens, it is equally important that we have a plan for the family meal. While the eating out plan seems the easy way to go, going to a fast food restaurant or some other quick food place does not demand as much respect as a home-cooked meal. Your children will see the time and love you put into the meals, and they will come to respect and appreciate you for it much more than a trip to McDonald's—not to mention the fact that a home-cooked meal is a much healthier option.

I know a home-cooked meal is a lot more work than a trip through the drive-thru, but it is a lot easier on our budget, and the 4:00 "what's for dinner" question won't seem so stressful if we have a plan. Moms for America has provided some great resources on the Home Reliance section of our website to help you as you form your plan and implement your Family Dinner Hour.

There is great value in a plan for all those involved, and it will make the dinner hour much more enjoyable for everyone.

If we are frustrated because we, once again, don't know what to make for dinner, our children will feel our frustration, and that frustration will inevitably carry over to the meal. But if we can take the time to decide what's for dinner, even before we make breakfast, then the decision is already made by the time dinner hour rolls around, and we will already have ensured we have the ingredients we need to make it—thus avoiding those last minute trips to the store which invariably make dinner late.

I made a habit several years ago of planning a two-week menu, and that little menu has been a huge blessing. It has taken so much stress off of me. I spend an hour going through the list of meals we frequently eat, throw in a few curves just for me, and then with a slide of the mouse and a click of a button, voila! I have a two-week dinner menu hot off the printer. I use that dinner menu when creating my grocery list, so I know when I go to make a meal, I'll have everything I need for it.

Making a menu has not only eliminated the stress of the 4:00 "what to make for dinner" panic, it has also saved a lot of money on our grocery bill. And the cool thing about the menu is that I can be flexible with it. If we have an activity one night and I have planned a meal that takes a lot of time to prepare, I just switch it with another night.

I can't tell you how freeing it is to have a plan, and it's not that hard to come up with one. You know better than anyone what your family likes to eat, so start there. Just make a list of meals your family likes—your "frequency list"—and that is where you begin. You don't have to make a whole two-week menu; you can just do one week. I usually make about 2/3 of my menu meals from my "frequency list," and then I add new things to try or a meal that I like even when it isn't necessarily a family favorite. For those meals, I add things on the side to ensure our children eat healthy things, like sliced cucumbers, canned fruit, and whole grain breads.

Another great idea when preparing the family meal is to include your children. Not only is it a good opportunity to share necessary skills with them, it is a great way to spend one-on-one time with your children.

When preparing dinner becomes an experience instead of a chore you are setting the tone and creating an atmosphere for a positive experience at the dinner table. Remember, you're not just making a meal, you are creating a venue for your family to gather where seeds of virtue, liberty, and patriotism can be sown and nurtured, and where love is expressed and relationships are fostered. As mothers and makers of the home, we can be a powerful force for strengthening our families when we use mealtimes to gather loved ones together.

As Julie Beck so eloquently stated, mothers "follow the example of the Savior to calm, teach, and help their families remember important things as they feed, cultivate, educate, and rear at the consecrated tables in their homes."

Kind of puts things in perspective, doesn't it?

Four: Sit Down to Dinner

It may seem a little ridiculous to add sitting down to eat as an actual "step" to family dinner, but in talking to many of my friends, this often seems to be the hardest part of the process, especially if you have teenagers who are used to eating on the run and spending as little time with family as possible. Actually sitting down together as a family is the *most* important part of the process; it demonstrates our commitment to each other and reminds us just how important our family is.

The second reason why this is the most important part of family dinner is because it provides us with the opportunity to pause from our busy lives and express gratitude. And what a powerful thing that is! It has been proven that a grateful heart not only makes us happier, it actually promotes good health and aids in the digestive process. A grateful heart is like medicine for the soul. How much better do we appreciate and enjoy our meal when we take the time to realize what a blessing it is to even have it and express gratitude from whence it came? There is nothing like taking a moment to thank God for our food and asking His blessing upon it. And what about the hands that prepared the food, and the hearts, bodies, and minds which labored to provide it? It sets just the right tone to begin the family meal.

It is much harder for us to complain or focus on what we *don't* have when we take the time to express gratitude for what we *do* have.

I will never forget the prayer our youngest offered one day as we sat down to family dinner. He was just five years old at the time. We had become accustomed to his sweet little simple prayers "Dear Father, thank you for the food. Amen." But he had apparently been listening all those years as his older brothers and sisters had taken their turns and given the blessing for that day, he seemed to take everything he had ever heard in a prayer and poured it all out in his sweet little words. He expressed thanks for the food, for the hands that prepared it, for his father who worked so hard to provide it, for the table to eat it on, the house to provide shelter, and a whole list of other things. When he finally said "Amen" his older brother looked over at him said, "Man you sure are thankful for a lot of things." To which Ethan responded, "Yes, I really am."

It was so cute; such a precious prayer, and it caused us all to reflect a little more on our blessings and make a special effort to show more gratitude for them.

We are expressing gratitude for our family simply by taking the time to sit down and eat together. When we take the time to put everything else aside, put the electronics away, postpone the homework, and adjust our schedules to actually sit down together, we are showing our children by our very actions just how important they are to us, and how grateful we are for them.

The third reason why sitting down together is the most important part of the Family Dinner Hour is because it gives us an opportunity to teach and nurture good manners. The family meal is a very powerful way to promote liberty and sustain a free society through the manners and etiquette our children develop as we eat dinner together.

When a society upholds a set of manners, it promotes a level of respect and understanding for others. The condition of civility in modern society has seriously declined in the past few decades, and this is due in great part to the deterioration of the Family Dinner Hour. It has become an unfortunate cycle. Because we stopped teaching and encouraging manners at the dinner table, our society has become less civil and the general population has a lower threshold of embarrassment, and that has led us to pay less attention to dining details. People have lost the sense of pride that comes with acting respectfully and politely at the dinner table, which, in prior generations, governed households in America. Because of this decline in our culture, we have become very poor communicators.

As one article expressed, "While technology has rapidly increased in other forms of communication, body language has been lacking in modern society. People still communicate nonverbally with their body language, they just care less about the message they are sending. Manners have been transformed over the years from a critical focus of meal time, to barely a concern for family dinners today."[3]

There are a lot of books on etiquette and manners in general as well as manners and etiquette at the table, and you can certainly refer to those books and resources when determining etiquette and manners at your own table, but I like to take a different approach. Rather than pour through Emily Post's "Rules of Etiquette" I use the "end from the beginning" approach. I think of the kind of adults I want my children to become—respectful, polite, considerate of others, etc.—and I create my rules of etiquette based on that. I consider what things

I can do to promote and nurture those kinds of behaviors, and we do those things.

I couldn't care less if my children have their elbows on the table or blow on their soup, but I do care that they learn patience as the food is passed around the table; that they learn courtesy when asking to have food passed to them rather than reaching for it; that they learn politeness by asking to be excused; that they learn respect for others' time and efforts by thanking those who prepared the meal. These are some of the things that are important to me, but what really matters is what is important to you.

Your list will be uniquely your own, meeting the needs, desires, and goals of your own family, but please, do take the time to teach and nurture these virtues. It would be a shame to waste such an incredible opportunity to cultivate a spirit of civility in the hearts and minds of those young patriots who will one day sit in halls of Congress, operate businesses, serve in communities, participate in elections, and carry on the torch of liberty and virtue for future generations.

Five: Open a Discussion

Dinner is as much about the conversation as it is about the meal, but it's not always easy for families to open up and talk to each other. That is why we have created this sampler of 31 Days of conversation starters, as well the additional ideas and resources we suggest. And while family dinner is a venue to cultivate the art of communication, it's not always necessary to have in-depth, revealing conversations with each other. It can just be a time to share funny stories or play a table game like "I Remember When..." or "Once upon a time..." These are two very simple games played somewhat alike.

I Remember When is played by one member of the family starting the sentence and adding an event they remember. Such as, "I remember when Grandpa took me fishing", "I remember when it snowed in April", "I remember when we left mom at the truck stop on the way to Mt. Rushmore" (this really happened to me). This game becomes very interesting when you add grandparents and older friends and relatives; "I remember when milk was delivered in bottles on our front porch", "I remember when gasoline was 25 cents a gallon". Oh the conversations memories like these can spark—and a lot of laughter too.

The second game, *Once Upon A Time*, is a game we played in the playground when I was a little girl. Someone starts a story beginning with "once upon a time" and it goes around the table as each person adds the next part of the story. We have had a lot of fun with this one.

Another idea that one of my friends does in her family is to share riddles and brainteasers. They have a collection of them, and when they have new people join them for dinner they love pulling out their favorites to see if their dinner guests can figure them out. Dinner time is a great opportunity to share stories about ancestors, American history, or just a great story that promotes good character such as *The Boy Who Cried Wolf*. No matter what you do, the important thing is that you *do*, and that you joy in doing it.

Six: Relax and Enjoy the Meal

It is a fact universally acknowledged that the American people eat too rapidly for the good of their health, and there is nothing that checks rapid eating like fun and merry conversation. I have already shared some ideas of how to open the conversation, but I want to focus on the "enjoy" part of the meal.

The Family Dinner Hour should be, and always remain, something everyone enjoys. Some of the conversation starters suggested in this booklet could easily lend to a lecture session if we are not careful, and we need to be *very* careful that it never does. Where is the enjoyment in knowing that every time you sit down to dinner you are going to get a lecture about how you need to do better or be better? Dinner time should be that small spot of peace, fellowship, and refuge for the entire family; it should *feel* safe.

Each member of the family should feel valued and be allowed to express their thoughts freely. The family is the first society, and it should be a society that nurtures character, not one that crushes it. So we need to take extra care to ensure that no family member becomes the target of ridicule or that their tender hearts are wounded at the expense of a joke. Parents set the tone at the table just as they do in the home itself. Children will follow our example, so we need to be sure that the behaviors and attitudes we are displaying are the same ones we want to see reflected back to us.

Family dinner should be a time where we can relax and enjoy the meal together. Stress is not good for the digestive system, but a feeling of merriment actually assists the digestive function—and it creates an environment of enjoyment. Your commitment will become much easier as your children actually look forward to Family Dinner Hour and no longer grumble that they have to leave their video game, their iPod, or their friends to eat dinner with their family.

Now I will address the "relax" part. Slowing down is not only good for conversation, it is good for your body. It actually makes you healthier, and helps you lose and/or maintain your weight. The digestion process tends to be a little slower than we are used to in our rushed and hurried lives. It takes 15 to 20 minutes for our bodies to realize we are full. So it stands to reason that if we have a full plate and eat everything on it in ten minutes, we will put more food on our plate because we won't know we are full. Maybe we were full when we ate only half of what was on our plate, but we are so busy eating we have no idea. An overfull belly is not good for our digestive systems—especially so close to bedtime. But if we slow down, converse in between bites, and consciously take 15 to 20 minutes to eat our meal, we will be better able to gage when our stomachs are full, we will feel better, maintain a healthier weight, and the whole digestion process will go much more smoothly.

Seven: Clean Up as a Family

I remember the first time I cooked a meal for my husband after we were married. When he was finished eating, he thanked me for the meal then got up and took his dishes to the kitchen. Then, as I brought my dishes into the kitchen, I found him rolling up his sleeves.

"Do you want to wash or dry?" he said. I was completely befuddled. I had no idea what to say. That may seem crazy to you, but when I was growing up, it was made very apparent from an early age that dishes was "women's work". So, I just assumed that I would clear the table and take care of the dishes while my husband did, well, whatever husbands do while you're doing the "women's work". But that very first day everything changed.

As I stood in the kitchen pondering my husband's question I immediately began to protest.

"I'll take care of the dishes," I said. "You just go and sit down."

"Are you going to come and sit down?" my husband asked.

"No, I'm going to do the dishes."

"Well, then I am going to do the dishes."

"But..." I stammered.

"But what?" he asked.

"But, it's my job."

"Why is it your job? You made dinner. We both ate it.

If anything, it should be my job. You made dinner after all. You shouldn't have to do the dishes too."

I had no idea what to say to that. It made perfect sense, sort of. So I picked up a dish towel and said, "I guess I'll dry."

And that started a tradition in our family that has carried on for almost thirty years and raised a lot of very respectful young patriots.

Over the years, we tried different methods of cleaning the kitchen from assigning specific chores to doing it together, and I can say that by far the best, most effective, most efficient, and most enjoyable method is for everyone to clean up after the meal together. In fact, we have a rule in our house that anyone who leaves the kitchen before asking what "their part" is has to do the dishes all by themselves. That has only happened twice in twenty years. I guess they needed the second time to see if we were really serious and would remember—we were, and we did.

Family cleanup is also a wonderful, extended opportunity for conversation and quality time. In our home, after the meal, everyone leaves the table, clears their dishes, and asks my husband or I what their part is. We divide the parts evenly, making an effort to ensure that the assignments rotate so everyone gets a chance to learn each skill from clearing the table to loading the dishwasher and sweeping the floor.

As the children have grown older, my husband has set a great example for them. He is always right in there cleaning with them. One day, my daughter asked why I wasn't helping in the kitchen. It just so happened that I was on the phone or I *would* have been helping, but I overheard my husband say, "because your mother made dinner. She shouldn't have to make dinner and clean the kitchen."

The next day my daughter asked if she could help with dinner. I was taken aback by the offer but I said, "Sure I'd love your help." Then her motive surfaced. "If I help with dinner," she asked, "does that mean I don't have to help clean the kitchen?"

"Sure," I said. "That sounds fair to me." And voila! A new tradition was born. Suddenly, I had a waiting list of helpers to help me with dinner. Only one person could help at a time, of course, otherwise no one would be left to clean the kitchen ☺

On another occasion, when we were cleaning up after dinner, one of my sons came to up to me as I was clearing the table and said, taking the plate from my hands, "Mom, you made dinner, you shouldn't have to clean the kitchen. I'll take care of that."

In the last ten years, I've only done the dishes a handful of times. I have six sons who won't let me. But I still like helping with the dinner clean up because I wouldn't want to miss those amazing conversations and that precious time with my family I so dearly cherish.

So, I would encourage you to consider the family clean-up plan. We are mothers, not maids. Our children need to understand that each person in the family needs to do their part in contributing to the home and family. Cleaning up together is a great way to teach the value of work and appreciation for those who do that work. It also causes our children to be conscientious about cleaning up after themselves. When everyone has ownership in the responsibility, each person is more likely to do their share.

I remember coming in the kitchen one day to hear my 10 year-old son say to my 6 year-old son, "Do you think someone is just going to come by and put that peanut butter away for you? If you leave that out, you're making more work for mom, and she does enough work."

My little six year-old, with a broken heart and tears welling up in his eyes said, "I'm sorry. I'll put it away."

And then his brother touched his little brother's tears, put his arm around his shoulder, and said, "It's okay, I'll help you."

Call me crazy, but I know that is a result of our family clean-up after dinner—a very important part of our Family Dinner Hour. And the best part of all is when everyone works together to clean up after dinner, EVERYONE gets to leave the kitchen to enjoy the evening. No one is left isolated in the kitchen with the tedious task of cleaning it alone, and we all enjoy and appreciate the clean-up time so much more. It is less stressful because we do not constantly need to go back in the kitchen and fuss at the children to get the dishes done—they *are* done!

And because the kitchen is done, we are in a joyful mood, and we have more time in the evening to spend doing the things we want to do. We have more reading time, more playing time, and more family time. And that is so worth it!

The Power of Family Dinner Hour: Reprise

I have shared a lot of information and ideas to get you started on your family dinner venture. It is my hope that you have found the information helpful, that I have adequately expressed the power and influence of the Family Dinner Hour, and that you have been inspired to begin, or continue, this family tradition in your home. It is our goal to help and support you in any way that we can.

We hope the resources in this book will be of help, and we hope you will share your ideas and experiences with us as well. We would love to hear from you and post your comments, suggestions, and ideas on our site for everyone to benefit from.

Let me conclude with these final thoughts and words of encouragement from Miriam Weinstein, author of *The Surprising Power of Family Meals*, who says, "If we want our kids to lead healthier lives, we should eat with them more often. We should talk to them. We should not give up our close contact, or underestimate our influence. And we should not pull back as they enter their teen years."[4]

It is never too late to sit down to dinner together, and there is no age limit. Our teens need that time just as much as our little ones. And the memories we make at our table will be held fondly in the hearts of our children for years, bringing them back to that table at holidays and special occasions when they're grown and have their own families.

And isn't that, after all, what it's all about?

Resources for Family Dinner Hour

Please help support our efforts by ordering products from our online store at HomeMakersforAmerica.org or through Amazon Smile. You can sign up through our website. When you order through our Amazon Smile, we receive a portion of your purchase and that allows to continue to provide the valuable support and resources you have come to count on every penny we receive is a treasure and we greatly appreciate your support.

Great Stories for the Dinner Table

- American History Stories by Mara L. Pratt—From the Freedom Series (available from Libraries of Hope.)

This is an amazing book full of short history stories your family will treasure. The stories are captivating enough to keep the attention of kids of all ages, and the events and people you will read about will inspire an even deeper love and appreciation for America. If you are looking for stories that will promote faith, virtue, and patriotism, this book is it.

- Restoring the Art of Story Telling in the Home (available through Libraries of Hope and Amazon Smile)

This whole book is outstanding. The first part talks about the power of a story and the art of storytelling, and the second part—the bulk of the book—is full of stories of adventure, fantasy, and even your favorite fairy tales. The beauty of this book is that each story is written in a short, simple way so that it can be read and then retold. What a great way to develop the art of storytelling and touch the heart of a child—just tell a story a day at the dinner table. (Great for bedtime too.)

- Remembering the Ladies by Kimberly and Cassiopeia Fletcher (available on Amazon and the Moms for America store)

This is an amazing book about the stories of women in the Revolution. Families will thoroughly enjoy the stories of the women who contributed and sacrificed so much for the dream of freedom. As a bonus, at the end of each story is information on memorials and historic sites you can visit that are associated with the people and events of the story.

- Story Bible (available at through Libraries of Hope LibrariesofHope.com)

Inspired by the recommendations of 19th Century British educator, Charlotte Mason, the Story Bible helps parents introduce the beautiful language of the King James Version to their children, while sharing the inspiring stories that have blessed Americans for so many years. The Story Bible features the simple stories of the Bible in chronological order providing a high-interest read-aloud for children while laying the perfect foundation for liberty. A must-have resource for every home, and great reading for the dinner table.

- History Stories for Children by Dr. John W. Wayland (available on Amazon Smile)

This classic is a full of little-known American history stories that children of all ages will enjoy—and parents will love to share them over and over.

- Choice Stories for Children selected by Ernest Lloyd (available on Amazon Smile)

A beautiful little book full of wonderful stories that promote faith, virtue, and patriotism—a collection of character classics.

Principles of Liberty for the Dinner Table

The 5000 Year Leap (available from The National Center for Constitutional Studies)

This is a fantastic book that presents the 28 Principles of Liberty our nation was founded on. It is a very easy read and organized in a way that you can read one principle a day and discuss it. Another option is to have everyone read a principle prior to dinner and then discuss the principle during dinner. Or for younger children, you can read the principle ahead of time and then share it with them using examples and stories they can relate to. Be careful however, not to assume they are too young to get something. You'd be surprised at what they grasp and what they remember.

- Catechism on the Constitution of the United States

("From the original 1828 Edition by Arthur J. Stansbury.) Available at the Moms for America webstore.)

This little book is a real treasure. It is full of simple questions and answers on the Constitution that are easy for all, any age, to understand. It is a great way to learn about the United States, the Constitution, and the principles of liberty that formed our nation. Lots of fun at the dinner table as a trivia game to find out how much we know about our country and learn more as we go.

- Promises of the Constitution by Pamela Romney Openshaw (available on Amazon or direct from the author)

Promises of the Constitution *is an outstanding resource for learning the Constitution, the history surrounding it, and the ways in which it has become twisted and ignored today. The book is written in clear, powerful 550 word vignettes on 129 topics that can be easily read in 3-5 minutes (perfect Family Dinner Hour)* Promises *is enjoyable to read and makes it simple to learn the history and inspired principles of the Constitution.*

---

1. Laurie David, "The Family Dinner"

2. Our Home, by C.E. Sargent, originally published 1883, republished by Archive Publishers

3. Tracing American Manners from Colonial Times through the 21st Century, December 9, 2011

4. Miriam Weinstein, The Surprising Power of Family Meals, 36 (Steerforth Publishing, 2006)

Day 1~ Share a Story

The Boy Who Cried Wolf

The Boy Who Cried Wolf

There once was a shepherd boy who was bored as he sat on the hillside watching the village sheep. To amuse himself he took a great breath and sang out, "Wolf! Wolf! The Wolf is chasing the sheep!"

The villagers came running up the hill to help the boy drive the wolf away. But when they arrived at the top of the hill, they found no wolf. The boy laughed at the sight of their angry faces.

"Don't cry 'wolf', shepherd boy," said the villagers, "when there's no wolf!" They went grumbling back down the hill.

Later, the boy sang out again, "Wolf! Wolf! The wolf is chasing the sheep!" To his naughty delight, he watched the villagers run up the hill to help him drive the wolf away.

When the villagers saw no wolf they sternly said, "Save your frightened song for when there is really something wrong! Don't cry 'wolf' when there is NO wolf!"

But the boy just grinned and watched them go grumbling down the hill once more.

Later, he saw a REAL wolf prowling about his flock. Alarmed, he leaped to his feet and sang out as loudly as he could, "Wolf! Wolf!"

But the villagers thought he was trying to fool them again, and so they didn't come.

At sunset, everyone wondered why the shepherd boy hadn't returned to the village with their sheep. They went up the hill to find the boy. They found him weeping.

"There really was a wolf here! The flock has scattered! I cried out, "Wolf!" Why didn't you come?"

An old man tried to comfort the boy as they walked back to the village.

"We'll help you look for the lost sheep in the morning," he said, putting his arm around the youth. "Nobody believes a liar...even when he is telling the truth!"

Additional Stories:

Another great story like this to share is from chapter 11 "The Harvest" in the book <u>Little House in the Big Woods</u> by Laura Ingalls Wilder. Laura's cousin Charley learns a valuable lesson.

Adaptations:

An idea for families with older children is to have *them* tell the story. This is also a good way to find out if they've even heard the story before. In families with older and younger children, you have the older children tell the story and then you can start a discussion with the younger children asking questions like: What did you think of that story? Why do you think the townspeople didn't come? What is the difference between a joke and a lie? Why do you think it is important to tell the truth?

Notes

_____
_____
_____
_____
_____
_____
_____
_____
_____
_____

Day 2 ~ Share a Story

Share the story of your child's (children's) birth. All children love to hear the story of when they were born. It is a story that is uniquely their own, and there is always something unique about each story.

Notes

_____
_____
_____
_____
_____
_____
_____
_____
_____

Day 3~ Share a Quote

"Always do your best. What you plant now, you will harvest later." ~Og Mandino

You can use this quote to spark a discussion asking such questions as: What does it mean to plant now and harvest later? If you want a good harvest what should you plant?

Thoughts to consider:

- Gardening doesn't just apply to vegetables, what we plant in our hearts and minds will be what we harvest.

- There is computer term called GIGO. It means Garbage In Garbage Out. Basically, it means that when you program a computer, what you put in is what you get out. If you put in wrong or corrupt data, what you will get out is inaccurate and corrupt information. The program will not work correctly. Our minds are like computers. What we put into our minds be it music, movies, pictures, thoughts, etc. will be what comes out in our words and actions. If we put good in, good will come out.

- Proverbs 23:7 For as he thinketh in his heart, so is he.

- "As the plant springs from, and could not be without, the seed, so every act of a man springs from the hidden seeds of thought and could not have appeared without them." ~James Allen, from <u>As A Man Thinketh</u>, chapter one.

Notes

DAY 4~ ASK A QUESTION

WHAT IS THE DIFFERENCE between a right and a privilege?

This is a great opportunity to start a family discussion on the difference between rights and privileges within the home. For example, food, clothes, and shelter are a right whereas video games, toys, and iPods are privileges. Rights are guaranteed; privileges are earned. The discussion can carry on into discussing the role of government and the difference between rights and privileges as citizens. (see Principle #8 *Man's Unalienable Rights* from the 5000 Year Leap to aid in your discussion)

DAY 5~ SHARE A STORY

The Nobility of a Boy

(STORY ADAPTED FROM A story told by Margaret Eggleston in her book <u>The Use of the Story in Religious Education</u>)

There was once a young boy named David who lived in New York City in the early 1900's. He worked as an errand boy at a bank near his home. His job was very important to the family for his father had recently passed away, and he had a mother and sister at home who were ill and could not walk. David was the only one left to care for his mother and sister, and he was the sole support for them. It took every cent he could possibly earn to take care of their little family.

A few weeks after David's father's funeral, the doctor came to the house to check in on David's mother and sister. The doctor told David that unless he could get his mother to the country where there was plenty of fresh air, she would grow increasingly worse and may very well be gone by winter. David tried everything he could to find a way to send his mother and sister to the country, but there was no way. He made barely enough money to provide their basic needs; there was no money to pay for them to stay in the country, and no one to house them. David was broken hearted, and he felt helpless as he watched day after day as his mother grew less and less strong.

One day, while working at the bank, David was sweeping under a table when he found a roll of bills—a big roll, and he could see that some of them were yellow-backs. Now at that time, yellow-backs were a type of paper currency that was redeemable for gold coin. These were issued until the early 1900's and thought very valuable as they were able to be exchanged into precious metal on demand.

David scooped up the bills and started to head for the office of the bank president when he suddenly hesitated realizing what this money would mean.

"Just think," he thought, "of what these bills will do. They can send mother and Millie away for the whole summer and then they will be well. No one knows I have them, and they don't belong to the bank. They were on the floor with trash paper. I'm going to keep them. Finding is keeping, and they are mine."

So, David dropped the wad of bills into his front pocket, then his back pocket, then shifted them into his coat pocket. He felt sure that everyone could see them as he left the bank, but no one stopped him. All the way home he fingered the bills in his pocket, taking his hand in and out of the pocket and shifting the bills inside. When he arrived home he checked on his mother and sister and then walked to the cupboard in the hallway, opened the front drawer, and dropped the bills inside, closing the drawer with a hard thud.

An hour later David walked back into the bank and shuffled quickly through the front room making his way to the office of the bank president. Entering the office, he threw the bills on the desk and whispered, "I found these when I swept."

Then, with a cry of pain, he fled from the bank.

The next morning, David was back at the bank to do his work when he was called into the bank president's office. When David entered the room the bank president looked up from his desk and spoke.

"David," he said, "I wish you would tell me why you brought those bills back last night. I know why you wanted them and what they would have done for you and your family. No one knew you had them. Why did you bring them back?"

David leaned far over the desk and looked right in the eyes of the president of the bank.

"Sir," he said, "as long as I live, I have to live with myself, and I don't want to live with a thief."

A few days later, the mother and Millie went to the country but not alone. David went with them, and they spent the whole summer in the countryside—a gift from the bank to show their deep appreciation for the nobility of the boy.

Day 6~ Share a Quote

"Failure to plan on your part does not constitute an emergency on my part." ~Author unknown

What a great quote to spark family discussion on the importance of planning, respecting the time and talents of others, and being considerate of others. Planning can include such things as putting events/activities on calendar, using an alarm clock, scheduling rides for activities, holding family meetings to go over calendar items, etc.)

Notes

_____
_____
_____
_____
_____

Day 7~ Share a Story

Prepare for Rain

(This story is from the film *Facing the Giants*, it is an excellent movie to watch together as a family)

A coach of a high school football team was deeply discouraged with the challenges in his work and personal life. He was struggling and questioned why God had put him in the position he was in. He shared his frustrations with an older man visiting the school. The other man responded to him with a story.

"There were two farmers that desperately needed rain, and both of them prayed for it. However, only one went out and prepared his fields to receive it. Which one do you think trusted God to send the rain?"

The coach responded, "The farmer who prepared his fields."

Then the older man responded by saying, "Which one are you? God will send the rain when He is ready. You need to prepare your field to receive it."

Bible verses to consider:

- Psalms 22:4 (KJV) Our fathers trusted in thee; they trusted, and thou didst deliver them.

- Proverbs 28:25 (KJV) He that is of a proud heart stirreth up strife: but he that putteth his trust in the Lord shall be made fat.

- Psalms 118:8&9 (KJV) It is better to trust in the Lord than to put confidence in man. It is better to trust in the Lord than to put confidence in princes.

- Psalms 20:7 (KJV) Some trust in chariots, and some in horses: but we will remember the name of the Lord our God.

- Proverbs 3:5 (KJV) Trust in the Lord with all thine heart; and lean not unto thine own understanding.

Notes

_____
_____
_____
_____

DAY 8~ SHARE A QUOTE

A quote by Mahatma Gandhi:

The seven things that will destroy us are:

1. Wealth without work

2. Pleasure without conscience

3. Knowledge without character

4. Commerce without morality

5. Science without humanity

6. Worship without sacrifice

7. Politics without principle

Additional quotes to consider:

- "You must be the change you wish to see in the world." ~Mahatma Gandhi

- "It takes courage to grow up and become who you really are." ~e. e. cummings

- "It's not hard to make decisions when you know what your values are." ~Roy Disney

Notes

Day 9~ Ask a Question

Will you be the hero of your own story?

Sharing the story of Esther and/or David & Goliath in the Bible are great examples of others who were the heroes of their own story. *The story of David & Goliath can be found in the <u>Story Bible</u> pages 254-259, the story of Esther pages 386-392*

Notes

_____
_____
_____
_____
_____

DAY 10~ SHARE A STORY

When the Cold Wind Blows

THERE ONCE WAS A farmer who desperately needed a good farmhand to help with the harvest. One young man came and interviewed for the job. The farmer asked, "What are your qualifications?" The shy young man quietly answered, "I can sleep when the cold wind blows." The farmer didn't know what to make of the young man's curious reply, but since the farmer had no other options, the young man was hired.

Throughout the harvest season the farmer was puzzled by his worker's answer on that first day they met. Nevertheless, the young man worked hard, and that was enough for the farmer.

Unexpectedly, one evening when the Autumn leaves were falling, a cold northerly wind began to blow. It came suddenly, the first major winter storm. The farmer had been in town, and as he rushed back to the farm, the harsh winds were starting to howl. The farmer was in a panic. He quickly pulled on his heavy boots, grabbed his work coat and, as he rushed out the door, called to the young man, who was already in bed and fast asleep. As the farmer ran to the field where the tractor had been left to rust, it angered him that his young farmhand would sleep when there was so much to be done and so little time to do it.

The farmer cursed himself for not fixing the hole in the barn's roof, knowing full well the rain and snow would soon come. He wished he had called ahead to tell his young worker to herd the animals into the barn when it was still light. On he trudged, in the dark with his coat pulled tightly and his head bowed into the wind.

Not finding the tractor in the field where he had last seen it, the farmer slogged his way to the barn. There he found, inside, the animals all safe and secure. He found each stall supplied with clean hay; the leaky roof had been patched. In the shed was parked the tractor, dry and protected from the elements.

The farmer took off his hat and scratched his head in amazement. "Who could have done it?" Then, in an instant, he understood the young man's curious answer, "I can sleep when the cold winds blow."

DAY 11 ~ SHARE A BIBLE VERSE

MATTHEW 5:14-16 (KJV)

Ye are the light of the world. A city that is set on an hill cannot be hid. Neither do men light a candle and put it under a bushel, but on a candlestick; and it giveth light unto all that are in the house. Let you light so shine before men, that they may see your good works and glorify your Father which is in heaven.

Additional quotes & verses to consider

- "Evil is like a shadow. It has no real substance of its own, it is simply a lack of light. You cannot cause a shadow to disappear by trying to fight it, stamp on it, by railing against it, or any other form of emotional or physical resistance. In order to cause a shadow to disappear, you must shine light on it." ~Shakti Gawain

- John 3: 19-21 (KJV) And this is the condemnation, that light is come into the world, and men loved darkness rather than light, because their deedswere evil. For every one that doeth evil hateth the light, neither cometh to the light, lest his deeds should be reproved. But he that doeth truth cometh to the light, that his deeds may be made manifest, that they are wrought in God.

- "The moral principles and precepts contained in the Scripture ought to form the basis of all our civil constitutions and laws. All the miseries and evil men suffer from vice, crime, ambition, injustice, oppression, slavery, and war,[sic] proceed from their despising or neglecting the precepts contained in the Bible." ~Noah Webster

- "Our Constitution was made only for a moral and religious people. It is wholly inadequate to the government of any other." ~John Adams

Notes

Day 12~ Ask a Question

IF YOU CAN SPEND one month in any country in the world, what country would it be?

Why would you like to go there? What would you like to see and do while you were there? Who would you like to take with you?

Note: This is a great opportunity to pull out a map of the world and point out the places everyone mentions and see where they are in relation to America.

Notes

_____
_____
_____
_____
_____

DAY 13~ SHARE A STORY

The Capture of Fort Ticonderoga

(STORY FROM THE FREEDOM Series, American History Stories Volume 1 by Mara L. Pratt)

In Vermont, called...the Green Mountain state, the men had formed themselves into a company under their colonel, Ethan Allen, and called themselves the Green Mountain Boys.

On the morning of the very day of the meeting of Congress which made George Washington Commander in Chief, Ethan Allen, with a detachment of these volunteers, set out to surprise Fort Ticonderoga.

Allen in a voice like thunder, so his followers say, demanded the instant surrender of the fort. The commander, frightened, and only half dressed, threw open his door, saying, 'By whose authority do you'—But Allen broke in upon him with, 'In the name of the Great Jehovah and the Continental Congress do I command you to surrender.'

No resistance was attempted; and so a large quantity of cannon and ammunition which the English had stored there, and which just then was so much needed by the troops at Boston, fell into the hands of the Americans, without the loss of a single man.

Notes

Day 14~ Ask a Question

Is WHAT'S RIGHT AND what's legal always the same thing?

Open a family discussion and share examples of when it is not. (Principle *#7 Equal Rights Not Equal Things* provides a good resource and example for this topic)

Notes

_____
_____
_____
_____
_____
_____
_____
_____
_____

DAY 15~ SHARE A STORY

Tall Tales *(An American tradition)*

A TALL TALE IS a story about a person who is larger than life. The descriptions in the story are exaggerated – much greater than in real life. This makes the story funny. Long ago, the people who settled in the wilderness areas of America first told tall tales. After a hard day's work, people gathered to tell each other funny stories. Paul Bunyan and Pecos Bill are some of the most famous tall tale characters.

Many years ago, Paul Bunyan was born in the northeastern American state of Maine. His mother and father were shocked when they first saw the boy. Paul was so large at birth that five large birds had to carry him to his parents. When the boy was only a few weeks old, he weighed more than fifty pounds.

As a child, Paul was always hungry. His parents needed ten cows to supply milk for his meals. Before long, he ate fifty eggs and ten containers of potatoes every day. Young Paul grew so big that his parents did not know what to do with him. Once, Paul rolled over so much in his sleep that he caused an earthquake. This angered people in the town where his parents lived. So, the government told his mother and father they would have to move him somewhere else.

Paul's father built a wooden cradle -- a traditional bed for a baby. His parents put the cradle in waters along the coast of Maine. However, every time Paul rolled over, huge waves covered all the coastal towns. So his parents brought their son back on land. They took him into the woods. This is where he grew up.

As a boy, Paul helped his father cut down trees. Paul had the strength of many men. He also was extremely fast. He could turn off a light and then jump into his bed before the room got dark.

Maine is very cold for much of the year. One day, it started to snow. The snow covered Paul's home and a nearby forest. However, this snow was very unusual. It was blue. The blue snow kept falling until the forest was covered.

Paul put on his snowshoes and went out to see the unusual sight. As he walked, Paul discovered an animal stuck in the snow. It was a baby ox. Paul decided to take the ox home with him. He put the animal near the fireplace. After the ox got warmer, his hair remained blue.

Paul decided to keep the blue ox and named him Babe. Babe grew very quickly. One night, Paul left him in a small building with the other animals. The next morning, the barn was gone and so was Babe. Paul searched everywhere for the animal. He found Babe calmly eating grass in a valley, with the barn still on top of his back. Babe followed Paul and grew larger every day. Every time Paul looked, Babe seemed to grow taller.

In those days, much of North America was filled with thick, green forests. Paul Bunyan could clear large wooded areas with a single stroke of his large, sharp axe. Paul taught Babe to help with his work. Babe was very useful. For example, Paul had trouble removing trees along a road that was not straight. He decided to tie one end of the road to what remained of a tree in the ground. Paul tied the other end to Babe. Babe dug his feet in the ground and pulled with all his strength until the road became straight.

In time, Paul and Babe the Blue Ox left Maine and moved west to look for work in other forests. Along the way, Paul dug out the Great Lakes to provide drinking water for Babe. They settled in a camp near the Onion River in the state of Minnesota.

Paul's camp was the largest in the country. The camp was so large that a man had to have one week's supply of food when walking from one side of the camp to the other. Paul decided to get other lumberjacks to help with the work. His work crew became known as the Seven Axemen. Each man was more than two meters tall and weighed more than one-hundred-sixty kilograms. All of the Axemen were named Elmer. That way, they all came running whenever Paul called them.

The man who cooked for the group was named Sourdough Sam. He made everything -- except coffee -- from sourdough, a substance used in making sourdough bread. Every Sunday, Paul and his crew ate hot cakes. Each hot cake was so large that it took five men to eat one. Paul usually had ten or more hot cakes, depending on how hungry he was. The table where the men ate was so long that a server usually drove to one end of the table and stayed the night. The server drove back in the morning, with a fresh load of food.

Paul needed someone to help with the camp's finances. He gave the job to a man named Johnny Inkslinger. Johnny kept records of everything, including wages and the cost of feeding Babe. He sometimes used nine containers of writing fluid a day to keep such detailed records.

The camp was also home to Sport, the Reversible Dog. One of the workers accidentally cut Sport in two. The man hurried to put the dog back together, but made a mistake. He bent the animal's back the wrong way. However, that was not a problem for Sport. He learned to run on his front legs until he was tired. Then, he turned the other way and ran on his back legs.

Big mosquitoes were a problem at the camp. The men attacked the insects with their axes and long sticks. Before long, the men put barriers around their living space. Then, Paul ordered them to get big bees to destroy the mosquitoes. But the bees married the mosquitoes, and the problem got worse. They began to produce young insects. One day, the insects' love of sweets caused them to attack a ship that was bringing sugar to the camp. At last, the mosquitoes and bees were defeated. They ate so much sugar they could not move.

Paul always gave Babe the Blue Ox a thirty-five kilogram piece of sugar when he was good. But sometimes Babe liked to play tricks. At night, Babe would make noises and hit the ground with his feet. The men at the camp would run out of the buildings where they slept, thinking it was an earthquake.

When winter came, Babe had trouble finding enough food to eat. Snow covered everything. Ole the Blacksmith solved the problem. He made huge green sunglasses for Babe. When Babe wore the sunglasses, he thought the snow was grass. Before long, Babe was strong and healthy again.

One year, Paul's camp was especially cold. It was so cold that the men let their facial hair grow very long. When the men spoke, their words froze in the air. Everything they said remained frozen all winter long and did not melt until spring.

Paul Bunyan and Babe left their mark on many areas. Some people say they were responsible for creating Puget Sound in the western state of Washington. Others say Paul Bunyan and Babe cleared the trees from the states of North Dakota and South Dakota. They prepared this area for farming.

Babe the Blue Ox died in South Dakota. One story says he ate too many hot cakes. Paul buried his old friend there. Today, the burial place is known as the Black Hills.

Whatever happened to Paul Bunyan? There are lots of theories. Some people say he was last seen in Alaska, or even the Arctic Circle. Another story says he still returns to Minnesota every summer and that Paul moves in and out of the woods so frequently that few people ever know that he is there. Who knows, maybe one day you might run in to Old Paul.

Notes

DAY 16~ SHARE A QUOTE

The American's Creed

BY WILLIAM TYLER PAGE

I believe in the United States of America as a government of the people, by the people, for the people; whose just powers are derived from the consent of the governed, a democracy in a republic, a sovereign Nation of many sovereign States; a perfect union, one and inseparable; established upon those principles of freedom, equality, justice, and humanity for which American patriots sacrificed their lives and fortunes.

I therefore believe it is my duty to my country to love it, to support its Constitution, to obey its laws, to respect its flag, and to defend it against all enemies.

–Written 1917, accepted by the United States House of Representatives on April 3, 1918.

DAY 17~ SHARE A STORY

A Story of George Washington

(STORY FROM THE FREEDOM Series, American History Stories Volume 1 by Mara L. Pratt)

During the Revolution, George Washington was one day riding by a group of soldiers who did not know him. They were busily engaged in raising a beam to the top of some military works. It was a difficult task, and often the corporal's voice could be heard shouting, "Now you have it!" "All ready! Pull!"

Washington quietly asked the corporal why he didn't help them.

"Sir," corporal angrily replied, "do you not realize that *I* am a *corporal*?"

Washington politely raised his hat saying, "I did not realize it. Beg your pardon, Mr. corporal."

Then, dismounting his horse, General Washington himself fell to work and helped the men till the beam was raised. Before leaving he turned to the corporal and, wiping the perspiration from his face, said, "If ever you need assistance like this again, call upon Washington, your commander-in-chief, and I will come."

The confused corporal turned red, and then white, as he realized that this was Washington himself to whom he had been so pompous; and we hope he learned a lesson of true greatness.

Notes

Day 18~ Ask a Question

If Stan Lee made you a superhero, what superpowers would you want to have?

What would you do with your superpowers? How would you use them?

Notes

_____
_____
_____
_____
_____
_____
_____
_____
_____

DAY 19~ SHARE A STORY

The Story of the Lightbulb

(STORY TOLD BY DIETER *Uchtdorf, a German aviator &
commercial pilot)*

On a dark December night 36 years ago, a Lockheed 1011 jumbo jet crashed into the Florida Everglades, killing over 100 people. This terrible accident was one of the deadliest crashes in the history of the United States.

A curious thing about this accident is that all vital parts and systems of the airplane were functioning perfectly—the plane could have easily landed safely at its destination in Miami, only 20 miles (32km) away.

During the final approach, however, the crew noticed that one green light had failed to illuminate—a light that indicates whether or not the nose landing gear has extended successfully.

The pilots discontinued the approach, set the aircraft into a circling holding pattern over the pitch-black Everglades, and turned their attention toward investigating the problem.

They became so preoccupied with their search that they failed to realize the plane was gradually descending closer and closer toward the dark swamp below. By the time someone noticed what was happening, it was too late to avoid the disaster.

After the accident, investigators tried to determine the cause. The landing gear had indeed lowered properly. The plane was in perfect mechanical condition. Everything was working properly—all except one thing: a single burned-out lightbulb. That tiny bulb—worth about 20 cents—started the chain of events that ultimately led to the tragic death of over 100 people.

Of course, the malfunctioning lightbulb didn't cause the accident; it happened because the crew placed its focus on something that seemed to matter at the moment while losing sight of what mattered most.

Set your hearts on the things that matter most.

Discussion: What are the things the matter most in your life? What are the things that you think matter most in our family? What kinds of things can distract us from those things that matter most?

"The Story of the Lightbulb, or Losing Sight of What Matters Most" by President Dieter F. Uchtdorf

© By Intellectual Reserve, Inc. Used by permission.

Day 20~ Share a Bible Verse

Genesis 1: 26-27 (KJV): And God said, Let us make man in our image, after our likeness: and let them have dominion over the fish of the sea, and over the fowl of the air, and over the cattle, and over all the earth, and over every creeping thing that creepeth upon the earth. So God created man in his own image, in the image of God created he him; male and female created he them.

THIS IS A GREAT opportunity to teach your children that they are children of God and that we were created by Him, and everything we have comes from Him. Other great points to cover are that we were created in God's image, and we have "dominion" or "stewardship" over all the earth. That can bring up a great discussion as to what dominion means and the responsibility we have to care for the earth that the God entrusted to us.

Notes

Day 21~ Ask a Question

Would you rather live in the country or the city? In the mountains or on the beach? On a farm or in the woods? In a cottage or in a high-rise apartment? Manhattan, NY or Mississippi? Why?

Notes

_____
_____
_____
_____
_____
_____
_____
_____
_____

DAY 22~ SHARE A STORY

The Price of a Soul

(ADAPTED FROM A STORY *by Robert Gay*)

Matthew 16:26 "...what shall a man give in exchange for his soul."

When Bobby was a young , boy in 1961, he loved to go to the movies. His parents assigned him chores around the house and paid him an allowance for his work. He earned a little over 50 cents a week and would often use that money to go to the movies.

Back then, a movie ticket cost 25 cents for an 11-year-old. That left Bobby with 25 cents for his second favorite thing—candy bars. Each candy bar cost 5 cents each. After buying the 25 cent movie ticket he had enough money to buy five whole candy bars! It was a boy's dream, and everything went well until he turned 12.

The price of the movie ticket for a 12 year-old was 35 cents—10 cents more. That would mean he could only buy three candy bars instead of the five he could buy when the ticket was only 25 cents.

On an afternoon following his birthday, Bobby was standing in line at the movie theater. As he walked through line watching all the 11 year-olds pay 25 cents for the ticket, he realized he didn't look any older than they did.

"I look the same as I did a week ago," Bobby reasoned with himself. He held his money in his hand and thought of the candy bars he could buy with that extra 10 cents.

As Bobby stepped up to the ticket booth he held out a quarter and asked for a 25-cent ticket. The cashier did not blink as he took the quarter and handed Bobby his ticket. Bobby triumphed at his brilliant success. He had a 25-cent ticket and 25 cents left to buy his regular five candy bars instead of three.

After the movie, still elated by his accomplishment, Bobby rushed home to tell his dad about his big coup. As Bobby poured out the details, his father said nothing. Then, when Bobby finished, his father simply looked at him and said, "Son, would you sell your soul for a nickel?"

His words pierced Bobby's 12-year-old heart. It is a lesson he has never forgotten.

The next week, Bobby went to back to the movie theater and with a grateful, repentant heart, handed the attendant 45 cents and left the theater with one candy bar.

Notes

DAY 23~ SHARE A STORY

"Give Me My Son!"

~Hannah Hendee

A TRUE STORY OF the Royalton Vermont Raid, October 16, 1780

Hannah Hendee was an extremely courageous woman and well deserving of the title of heroine. In 1780, a messenger from the neighboring Vermont town where Hannah and her husband lived with their two small children came to warn them that Indians were raiding the area under the leadership of the British Army. Hannah's town was next in their path.

Hannah's husband told her to take their young son and baby daughter to a neighbor's house and hide there until the raids were over. He then rode out to warn the next town. On the way to her neighbor's house, Hannah was overcome by a band of Indians who rode by and ripped her seven-year-old son, Michael, right from her hands.

Hannah, holding her daughter in her arms, immediately ran after the vicious mob that stole her son, but they were too fast for her. Resolute in her mission to rescue her son, Hannah followed the Indians' path of destruction and burning homes until she finally reached the British camp where they had originated. Hannah's son and several other boys were huddled together in the encampment surrounded by several Indians.

Hannah, upon finding the British officer in charge, walked up to him and demanded the release of her son. The officer, Lieutenant Horton, explained that the boys were payment to the Indians and that they would not be killed but taken to Canada and trained to become Indian Warriors.

"No child will be able to endure the long trek back to Canada!" Hannah cried. "They will die before you reach there! Have you no mercy? Have the British become such savages that they murder children?" Hannah then pleaded, "Give me my son. Don't let him die."

Lt. Horton finally relinquished her son, but Hannah didn't stop there. After securing her son's safe release, Hannah looked around at the terrified, desolate group of boys and declared she would be taking them as well. When Lt. Horton protested, Hannah was steadfast and relentless in her determination to free and return every one of the boys who had been stolen from their families in the raids.

Lt. Horton finally relented and allowed Hannah to take all the boys. Still holding her baby in her arms, Hannah pulled the small, scared, and crying boys in around her skirts and walked them back to the town where they were reunited with their families.

Notes

Day 24~ Share a Quote

"It is our choices...that show who we really are, far more than our abilities."

~J.K. Rowling

ADDITIONAL QUOTES FOR CONVERSATION:

- "Life is not about learning how to avoid the storms. It's about learning how to dance in the rain."~Anonymous

- "Challenges are what make life interesting; overcoming them is what makes life meaningful."~Anonymous

- "The only thing necessary for the triumph of evil is for good men to do nothing." ~Edmund Burke

DAY 25~ SHARE A STORY

Team Hoyt

RICK WAS BORN IN 1962 to Dick and Judy Hoyt. As a result of oxygen deprivation to Rick's brain at the time of his birth, Rick was diagnosed as a spastic quadriplegic with cerebral palsy. Dick and Judy were advised to institutionalize Rick because there was no chance of him recovering and little hope for Rick to live a "normal" life.

"They told us to put Rick away in an institution," remembers Dick, "because they said he was going to be nothing but a vegetable for the rest of his life. We said, No, were not going to do that. We're going to bring Rick home and bring him up like any other child."

Dick and Judy soon realized that though Rick couldn't walk or speak; he was quite astute, and his eyes would follow them around the room. They fought to integrate Rick into the public school system, pushing administrators to see beyond Rick's physical limitations. Dick and Judy would take Rick sledding and swimming, and even taught him the alphabet and basic words like any other child. After providing concrete evidence of Rick's intellect and ability to learn like everyone else, Dick and Judy needed to find a way to help Rick communicate for himself.

In 1972, with $5,000 and a skilled group of engineers at Tufts University, an interactive computer was built for Rick. This computer consisted of a cursor being used to highlight every letter of the alphabet. Once the letter Rick wanted was highlighted, he was able to select it by just a simple tap with his head against a head piece attached to his wheelchair. When the computer was first brought home, Rick surprised everyone with his first words. Instead of saying, "Hi, Mom," or "Hi, Dad," Rick's first "spoken" words were: "Go, Bruins!" The Boston Bruins were in the Stanley Cup finals that season. It was clear from that moment on that Rick loved sports and followed the game just like anyone else.

In 1975, at the age of 13, Rick was finally admitted into public school. After high school, Rick attended Boston University and graduated with a degree in Special Education in 1993.

In the spring of 1977, at age 15, Rick told his father that he wanted to participate in a 5-mile benefit run for a Lacrosse player who had been paralyzed in an accident. Far from being a long-distance runner, Dick agreed to push Rick in his wheelchair, and they finished all 5 miles, coming in next to last.

That night, Rick told his father, "Dad, when I'm running, it feels like I'm not handicapped."

That message on Rick's makeshift computer began an odyssey of love that continues to this day, taking father and son to competitions around the world. Following that first race in 1977, Rick and his father Dick began participating in marathons and triathlons from Boston to Hawaii as Team Hoyt.

For more than 30 years, Dick has either towed, pushed, or carried Rick in a string of athletic challenges, including every Boston Marathon since 1981. In 2008, father and son participated and the strenuous Ironman Triathlon World Championships in Hawaii—the most prominent triathlon race in the world.

For that event, competitors have to swim 2 ½ miles through the ocean and then peddle a bicycle 112 miles before running a hilly, 26.2 mile marathon. In the triathlon swim, Rick lies on his back in a rubber raft attached by rope to a wetsuit vest worn by his father. In the bike portion, Rick sits in a chair attached to the front of Dicks bike, and on the run, Dick pushes Rick in the race chair.

The 2009, Boston Marathon was officially Team Hoyt's 1000th race. Rick always says if it comes down to doing one race a year he would like it to be the Boston Marathon: his favorite race. Dick Hoyt hopes that he is able to push Rick in the Boston Marathon when he is 70 years old.

Rick was once asked, if he could give his father one thing, what would it be? Rick responded, "The thing I'd most like is for my dad to sit in the chair, and I would push him for once."

Additional Resources and Information:

There are some amazing videos of Team Hoyt on YouTube. The jerry-rigged chair that Dick pushed Rick in during their very first race now resides in the Massachusetts Sports Hall of Fame.

Notes

DAY 26~ SHARE A BIBLE VERSE

JOSHUA 24:15

> And if it seem evil unto you to serve the LORD, choose you this day whom ye will serve; whether the gods which your fathers served that were on the other side of the flood, or the gods of the Amorites, in whose land ye dwell: but as for me and my house, we will serve the LORD.

Additional Quotes & Suggestions:

You can ask your children to share their favorite stories from the Bible where people chose the Lord. Some great stories to share are Moses, Daniel, and *Shadrach, Meshach, and Abednego.*

Those people who will not be governed by God will be ruled by tyrants.

~William Penn

Notes

DAY 27~ ASK A QUESTION

How can you show someone that they are special to you?

Notes

_____
_____
_____
_____
_____
_____
_____
_____
_____
_____
_____

Day 28~ Share a Story

The Emperor's New Clothes

By Hans Christian Anderson

Once upon a time there lived a vain Emperor whose only worry in life was to dress in elegant clothes. He changed clothes almost every hour and loved to show them off to his people. Word of the Emperor's refined habits spread over his kingdom and beyond. Two scoundrels who had heard of the Emperor's vanity decided to take advantage of it. They introduced themselves at the gates of the palace with a scheme in mind.

"We are two very good tailors," they said, "and after many years of research, we have invented an extraordinary method to weave a cloth so light and fine that it looks invisible. As a matter of fact, it is invisible to anyone who is too stupid and incompetent to appreciate its quality."

The chief of the guards heard the scoundrel's strange story and sent for the court chamberlain who told the Emperor the news. The Emperor's invited the scoundrels into his chamber.

The Scoundrels entered the room and bowed low before the Emperor. They confirmed the story the Emperor had been told and that the cloth was so light and magnificent that only the very wise and great could see it.

"Besides being invisible, your Highness," they said, "this cloth will be woven in colors and patterns created especially for you."

The emperor gave the two men a bag of gold coins in exchange for their promise to begin working on the fabric immediately.

The two scoundrels asked for a loom, silk, and gold thread which the Emperor ordered to be given them. Then the men set to work pretending to sew the beautiful cloth.

The Emperor thought he had spent his money quite well: in addition to getting a new extraordinary suit, he would discover which of his subjects were ignorant and incompetent. A few days later, he called the old and wise prime minister, who was considered by everyone as a man with common sense.

"Go and see how the work is proceeding," the Emperor told him, "and come back to let me know."

The prime minister was welcomed by the two scoundrels.

"We're almost finished," they said, "but we need a lot more gold thread. Here, Excellency! Admire the colors, feel the softness!"

The old man bent over the loom and tried to see the fabric that was not there. He felt cold sweat on his forehead.

"I can't see anything," he thought. "If I see nothing, that means I'm stupid! Or, worse, incompetent!"

The prime minister knew if he admitted that he didn't see anything, he would be discharged from his office. So he looked at the empty loom and said, "What a marvelous fabric. I'll certainly tell the Emperor."

The two scoundrels rubbed their hands gleefully. They had almost made it. More thread was requested to finish the work.

Finally, the Emperor received the announcement that the two tailors had come to take all the measurements needed to sew his new suit.

"Come in," the Emperor ordered. Even as they bowed, the two scoundrels pretended to be holding a large roll of fabric.

"Here it is your Highness, the result of our labor," the scoundrels said. "We have worked night and day but, at last, the most beautiful fabric in the world is ready for you. Look at the colors and feel how fine it is."

Of course the Emperor did not see any colors and could not feel any cloth between his fingers. He panicked and felt like fainting. But luckily, the throne was right behind him, and he sat down. But when he realized that no one could know that he did not see the fabric, he felt better. Nobody could find out he was stupid and incompetent. And the Emperor didn't know that everybody else around him thought the very same thing.

The farce continued as the two scoundrels had foreseen it. Once they had taken the measurements, the two began cutting the air with scissors while sewing with their needles an invisible cloth.

"Your Highness," they said, "you'll have to take off your clothes to try on your new ones." The two scoundrels draped the new clothes on him, and then held up a mirror. The Emperor was embarrassed, but since none of his bystanders were, he felt relieved.

"Yes, this is a beautiful suit, and it looks very good on me," the Emperor said trying to look comfortable. "You've done a fine job."

"Your Majesty," the prime minister said, "we have a request for you. The people have found out about this extraordinary fabric, and they are anxious to see you in your new suit."

The Emperor was doubtful about showing himself naked to the people, but then he abandoned his fears. After all, no one would know about it except the ignorant and the incompetent.

"All right," he said. "I will grant the people this privilege."

He summoned his carriage, and the ceremonial parade was formed. A group of dignitaries walked at the very front of the procession and anxiously scrutinized the faces of the people in the street. All the people had gathered in the main square, pushing and shoving to get a better look. An applause welcomed the regal procession. Everyone wanted to know how stupid or incompetent his or her neighbor was but, as the Emperor passed, a strange murmur rose from the crowd.

Everyone said, loud enough for the others to hear: "Look at the Emperor's new clothes. They're beautiful!" "What a marvelous train!" "And the colors! The colors of that beautiful fabric! I have never seen anything like it in my life!"

They all tried to conceal their disappointment at not being able to see the clothes, and since nobody was willing to admit his own stupidity and incompetence, they all behaved as the two scoundrels had predicted.

A child, however, who had no important job and could only see things as his eyes showed them to him, went up to the carriage.

"The Emperor is naked," he said.

"Fool!" his father reprimanded, running after him. "Don't talk nonsense!"

He grabbed his child and took him away. But the boy's remark, which had been heard by the bystanders, was repeated over and over again until everyone cried:

"The boy is right! The Emperor is naked! It's true!"

The Emperor realized that the people were right but could not admit to that. He thought it better to continue the procession under the illusion that anyone who couldn't see his clothes was either stupid or incompetent. So he stood stiffly on his carriage, nodding to the crowd, while a page held his imaginary mantle behind him.

DAY 29~ ASK A QUESTION

IF YOU COULD HAVE a zoo in your back yard but the City government would only allow you to have five animals, which five animals would you choose?

Additional Questions to consider:

- Why does the city government limit the number of animals? Is it a law? Can it be changed?

- Are there certain kinds of animals you are limited to or can you have any kind of animal as long as there are only five?

- Is it five of the same animal or five animals all together?

- Does the city have the authority to limit the number of animals you have?

DAY 30~ SHARE A STORY

The Landlord's Mistake

(STORY TAKEN FROM THE *"Stories of Great Americans"* volume of the *Freedom Series*)

When John Adams was president and Thomas Jefferson was Vice President of the United States there was not a railroad in all the world.

People did not travel very much. There were no broad, smooth highways as there are now. The roads were crooked and muddy and rough.

If a man was obliged to go from one city to another he often rode on horseback. Instead of a trunk for his clothing, he carried a set of saddle bags, instead of sitting at his ease in a parlor car, he went jolting along through the mud and mire, exposed to wind and weather.

One day, some men were sitting by the door of a hotel in Baltimore. As they looked down the street, they saw a horseman coming. He was riding very slowly, and both he and his horse were bespattered with mud.

"There comes old farmer mossback," said one of the men laughing, "he's just in from the backwoods."

"He seems to have a hard time of it," said another. "I wonder where he'll put up for the night."

"Oh any kind of place will suit him," answered the landlord. "He's one of those country fellows who can sleep with the haymow and eat with the horses."

The traveler was soon to the door. He was dressed plainly, and with his reddish brown hair and bespattered face, looked like a hard working countryman just in from the back woods.

"Have you a room here for me?" he asked the landlord.

Now the landlord prided himself upon keeping a first class hotel, and he feared that his guests would not like the look of the rough-looking traveler. So he answered, "No, sir. Every room is full. The only place I could put you would be in the barn."

"Well then," answered the stranger, "I will see what they can do for me at the planters tavern around the corner." And he rode away.

About an hour later, a well-dressed gentleman came into the hotel and said, "I wish to see Mr. Jefferson."

"Mr. Jefferson?" said the landlord.

"Yes sir, Thomas Jefferson, the Vice President of the United States."

"He isn't here."

"Oh, but he must be. I met him as he rode into town, and he said he intended to stop at this hotel. He has been here about an hour."

"No he hasn't. The only man that has been here for lodging today was an old clodhopper who was so spattered with mud that you couldn't see the color of his coat. I sent him 'round to Planters."

"Did he have reddish-brown hair, and did he ride a gray horse?"

"Yes, and he was quite tall."

"That was Mr. Jefferson," said the gentleman.

"Mr. Jefferson!" cried the landlord. "That was the vice president—here? Build a fire in the best room. Put everything in tip-top order, Sally. What a dunce I was to turn Mr. Jefferson away! He shall have all the rooms in the house, and the ladies parlor too, I'll go right 'round to the Planters and fetch him back."

So he went to the hotel where he found the Vice President sitting with some friends in the parlor.

"Mr. Jefferson," he said, "I have come to ask your pardon. You were so bespattered with mud that I thought you were some old farmer. If you'll come back to my house, you shall have the best room in it. Yes, all the rooms if you wish. Won't you come?"

"No," answered Mr. Jefferson. "A farmer is as good as any other man, and where there is no room for a farmer, there can be no room for me."

Day 31 ~ Share a Quote

"Happier than any fairy tale, more marvelous than any wonder book, the story of the United States of America begins, 'Once upon a time,' and has come to the point where it depends upon the boys and girls who read it to say whether or not they shall 'live happily ever after.'"

The True Story of Christopher Columbus, by Elbri

Notes

_____
_____
_____
_____
_____
_____
_____

Notes

www.ingramcontent.com/pod-product-compliance
Lightning Source LLC
Chambersburg PA
CBHW060206050426
42446CB00013B/3001